Psychic Empath

The Ultimate Guide to Psychic development, and to understand your Empath abilities.

Psychic awareness

Frank Knoll

Disclaimer

The author and publisher of this eBook have used their best efforts in preparing it. The author and publisher make no representation or warranties with respect to the accuracy, applicability, or completeness of the contents of this resource.

The information contained in this eBook is strictly for educational purposes. Therefore, if you wish to apply the ideas contained herein, you are taking full responsibility for your actions.

Trademarks mentioned in this book are property of their respective owners and may not be used without written permission. The fact that organizations, or websites are referred to in this work as examples does not mean that the author endorses the information, the company or website.

Readers should be aware that the information listed in this work may have changed or disappeared between when this book was written and when it is read.

Table of Contents

Introduction 1

Chapter 1 - What is an Empath? 3

Chapter 2 - Common Traits of an Empath 9

Chapter 3 - Surviving Emotional Vampires 18

Chapter 4 - Understanding Psychic Empaths 26

Chapter 5 - Shielding & Clearing your Energy 31

Conclusion 40

Introduction

This book has actionable information that will help you to increase your awareness effectively to get rid of stress and in an effort to be happy. Other books that have helped with these processes are: The Power of Focus and the Ultimate Morning Rituals.

I want to send you a big thank you for downloading the book, "Psychic Empath."

Empaths have rare and special gift. They are unique, intuitive, creative and most of all, they have the ability to feel what others feel. They are also highly psychic. They can communicate with nature and animals, and receive information from various objects. Many of them can sense the past, present and future states of the environment and the people in it. However, in exchange for these remarkable traits, many empaths suffer from too much negativity and find it difficult to cope with their empathic abilities.

If you're an empath or suspect that you are, this book will help you understand yourself better and teach you strategies on how to make the most out of your abilities. You will also learn many ways to protect yourself from all the negative vibrations out there. If you have a friend or a family member who is an empath, then you will appreciate them even more and know how to interact with them in a healthier way.

Thanks again for downloading this book, I hope you enjoy it!

Chapter 1 - What is an Empath?

An empath is a person who is affected by the energy of other people and has an intrinsic capacity to intuitively perceive and feel others. Unconsciously, our lives are influenced by others' wishes, desires, moods and thoughts. However, more than feeling emotions on a deeper level, empaths can also perceive spiritual urges and physical sensitivities, and sense the intentions and motivations of others.

Empaths are born, not made. Their abilities are genetic traits, inherent in their DNAs and are often passed through generations. This means being an empath is not something that you can learn. It's either you're an empath or not at all.

Being an empath means you're always open to process the energy and feelings of other people. In most cases, you take on those emotions as if they were your own. You feel as intensely as the person from whom you're absorbing the energy and emotions. For this reason, empaths often experience unexplained pains and aches, environmental sensitivities, chronic fatigue, and the like. These things can be attributed mostly to external influences and less to your inner self. You are essentially treading this earth with all the accumulated energies, karma and emotions from others.

Mostly, empaths are quiet achievers. These world-class nurturers can take a while to handle compliments because they are more inclined to identify the positive attributes of another person. They are exceptionally expressive in every aspect of emotional connection. They talk openly and quite frankly. However, they may find it difficult to discuss their own emotions no matter how much the other party cares to listen.

On the other hand, empaths can also be the unresponsive and reclusive type. They may even seem insensible. Some are good at "shutting out" others in an attempt to block the barrage of intense emotions coming from the external environment, and protect their own inner feelings.

Empaths tend to openly feel and become more conscious about what is outside than what is within them. This can make empaths disregard their own particular needs. Empath are generally non-aggressive and non-violent individuals. Most of the time, they act as the peacemaker. Any place or situation filled with chaos or disharmony creates an awkward, uncomfortable feeling in empaths.

In case they find themselves caught in the middle of an argument, they will strive to fix the issue as fast as possible, or avoid it altogether if they can. If any foul words or profane language is expressed in their defense, an empath is likely to resent his lack of discipline and self-control.

Many empaths are excellent storytellers because of their inquisitive minds, vast imagination, immense creativity and constantly expanding knowledge. They can be tender, sentimental and romantic at heart. They may also act as the "keepers" of family history and ancestral knowledge.

If not the apparent family historians, empaths may be the ones who attentively listen to the stories being passed down from generation to generation, so it is not surprising if they already possess or may have started a family tree.

Empaths have great interest in a wide variety of music to match their numerous expressive temperaments. Others can be puzzled at how empaths can listen to one music genre and switch to something completely different within minutes. Empaths pay close attention to the lyrics of songs. Words have powerful, adverse effects on them, especially if the song is relevant to their current situation or recent experience. In such cases, it is advisable for an empath to listen to music with no accompanying lyrics to avoid creating havoc in their emotional state.

An empath has a great tendency to pick up others' emotions and project them back without recognizing its source in the first place. For a learning empath, it is vital to talk things out in order to release emotions. Empaths ultimately develop a stronger, higher level of understanding, enabling themselves to find peace in any situation. The consequence to this is that they tend to bottle up their emotions and build sky-high barriers so as to not let other people know their deepest, innermost thoughts and feelings. This suppression of emotional expression can be one of the direct results of an expressionless upbringing, a traumatic experience, or perceiving the notion that "Children are only meant to be seen, not heard" early in their lives.

Most empaths are sensitive to news, TV, movies, broadcasts and videos. Violence and dramas portraying shocking scenes of emotional or physical pain inflicted on children, women, animals and adults can easily bring empaths to tears, although they try to hold back the tears at times.

Scenarios like these may also make them feel physically ill. Some empaths struggle in attempting to comprehend the need for such cruelty and violence. They may have difficulty expressing their thoughts and feelings in the presence of others who are ignorant, close-minded and lack compassion.

You will often find empaths working with nature, animals and other people with dedication, true passion and sincerity to help. Most of them are tireless teachers and caretakers of the environment. Many volunteers who do charitable work are empathic people. They give up their personal time without pay or recognition for the sake of helping those who are in desperate need.

Empaths are thinkers and problem-solvers. They also study various things. They will search untiringly until they find the answers and solutions to problems. This is particularly beneficial for building better relationships, enhancing the workplace and nurturing home life.

Many empaths are lucid dreamers and inquisitive of their dreams' content. They can see their dreams vividly and remember them in detail. Most of the time, they feel as if the dreams are somehow connected to their waking life and not just random mumbles of irrelevant and nonsensical images. This curiosity leads them to unravel the mystery behind their dreams and link the interpretation to its significance in their waking life. If not, empaths will find other means that will lead them to the interpretations of their dreams.

In all likelihood, empaths will have varying paranormal encounters over the course of their lives. OBEs (out of body experiences) and/or NDEs (near death experiences) can awaken an unaware empath and begin their journey towards discovery and better understanding of themselves.

For empaths without knowledge of their empathic/psychic capacities, the lack of understanding towards their paranormal experiences may suppress such abilities. Any empath who is going through this stage may need to pursue their interest in the paranormal or the "unexplained" to find explanations and accept (and embrace) their life circumstances.

Chapter 2 - Common Traits of an Empath

Are you a highly sensitive person? How do you feel when someone else is in pain? How do you react to violence? Do you often encounter unexplainable things and events? Your answers to these questions can determine whether or not you are an empath.

Below are 33 common traits an empath possesses:

1. Highly sensitive - An empath is naturally giving and spiritually open. If you want sincere heart, you can bet empaths have it. If they say they care, they genuinely do and will stand by you through ups and downs. They are also great listeners. They often do not talk about themselves that much unless it is to someone they truly trust. Since they're highly sensitive, empaths can have their feelings easily hurt, too.

2. Introverted - Empaths are mostly introverted. They tend to become overwhelmed in parties, crowds and public places, like stadiums, shopping malls and supermarkets. Being around a lot of people fills an empath with disorderly vexed emotions coming from others. As such, they usually prefer small groups or one-to-one contacts.

3. Creative - Empaths have vivid imagination and strong creative quality. They are mostly drawn to

various forms of art—from singing and dancing to acting, writing, painting and drawing.

4. Feels other people's emotions - Empaths absorb other's moods and emotions, both positive and negative, and take them on as their own. Taking on angry or anxious feelings can be exhausting for them while taking on love and peace helps them flourish. More adept empaths are capable of feeling emotions even from a great distance, allowing them to know if someone is thinking negatively about them without getting close.

5. Highly intuitive - An empath naturally develops intuition and experiences the world through their instinctive senses. They use their gut feelings to identify a person's intentions. This helps them find and build positive relationships, and steer clear of energy vampires.

6. Knows things without being told - This ability goes far beyond gut feelings or intuition, although that's how many people will explain it. Empaths simply know a lot of things without being told, sometimes even without the intention of knowing in the first place. The more attuned an empath is, the stronger his power of knowing becomes.

7. Unable to bear watching violence - Watching cruelty, tragedy or any kind of violence, in person or on TV, is intolerable for empaths. Some may

even find it unbearable to read comics or newspaper with too many violent scenarios. Eventually, this may make an empath stop reading the newspaper and watching TV altogether.

8. Has the ability to sense dishonesty - If a loved one or a friend is telling lies, an empath will know. However, since it can be painful to know an important person is lying, empaths try to divert their attention and not focus on the notion that they're being lied to. An empath will also feel and know when a person says one thing but thinks or feels another.

9. Picks up physical ailments off other people - More often than not, an empath will develop common ailments (colds, pains, body aches, eye infections, etc.) off other people, especially those they are closest to. Some refer to these as "sympathy pains".

10. Develops lower back and digestive problems - The "seat of emotions," or the solar plexus chakra, is located in the center of the abdomen. This is where an empath feels incoming emotions of other people. If the empath absorbs too much emotion, that specific area may weaken, leading to stomach ulcers and inflammatory bowel disorders (IBD). Problems in the lower back often arise out of being ungrounded, meaning the person is unaware of his/her being an empath.

11. Notices the underdog - Empaths have a way of identifying the underdog. Anyone who is suffering, either from being bullied or emotional pain, attracts an empath's compassion and attention.

12. Experiences constant fatigue - An empath's energy often gets drained due to taking on excessively from others or being targeted by energy vampires. This kind of fatigue cannot be simply cured by sleep.

13. Becomes a dumping ground of other people's problems - If you're an empath, other people, even strangers, will want to unload their personal problems and issues on you. If you're not careful enough, these problems can end up as your own.

14. Finds intimate relationships overwhelming - Empaths often find it difficult to deal with too much intimacy or togetherness. As such, they may intentionally avoid being in intimate relationships, in the fear of losing their identity and being engulfed. This is why most empaths choose to stay alone.

15. Tends to be addictive – To block out other people's emotions, empaths may turn to drugs, alcohol, sex, or other types of addiction. This is their way of protecting themselves and hiding from something or someone.

16. Interested in holistic therapies, healing, and anything metaphysical - Empaths have an inherent ability to heal others and are very keen on doing so. Despite that, they may turn away from being the healer once they've taken too much from the person they're trying to heal. This happens more often in empaths who have no knowledge of their abilities. Ultimately, empaths will be drawn to holistic therapies, healing, and everything metaphysical or of supernatural nature.

17. Loves nature and animals - Having pets is essential for empaths, so is being outdoors and one with nature. For the most part, these are ways for them to replenish lost energy.

18. Needs alone time - Always being around people can be exhausting for empaths so they occasionally need solitude and quiet time to recharge. They need even just a short escape from the mundane to prevent emotional overload.

19. Gets bored easily - Whether at home, in school, or at work, things have to be kept stimulating and interesting for empaths, otherwise they can easily get distracted and end up doodling or daydreaming. Doing something they don't like makes an empath feel like he's living a lie, and labelling them as lazy for being that way will only make them unhappy. This is why many empaths are often seen as idle or lazy people.

20. Has highly tuned senses - Due to their highly tuned senses, empaths' nerves can get easily frayed by excessive talking, loud noises and strong smells. This is another reason empaths constantly seek quiet and solitude.

21. Free-spirited - While mostly introverted, empaths are free-spirited individuals. They love travel, freedom and adventure. Setting restrictions and taking away their freedom can be debilitating, even poisoning, to an empath.

22. Dislikes clutter - Clutter and disorderly things block the flow of energy, making an empath feel heavy and weighed down. As such, empaths strive to maintain neatness in their environment, so they can breathe and keep the energy flowing freely.

23. Loves daydreaming - An empath can literally stare into blankness for several hours, being blissfully happy in their own little world. This is perhaps where some of their creative ideas are born.

24. Strives to look for answers, knowledge and the truth - Empaths are always in search of new knowledge and answers to questions that they may encounter. To have an unanswered question can be frustrating, thus an empath strives to find an explanation and seek confirmation for the things they already know. This, however, often leads to information overload.

25. Frequently experiences synchronicities and déjà vu - What may initially appear as mere coincidences will ultimately lead to an empath's understanding that synchronicities are essential aspects of their being. As the understanding of one's self grows, these synchronicities will become more fluent, free-flowing and with expanding occurrence.

26. Finds rules and routines imprisoning - An empath is not likely to stay long in a place where there are too many rules to follow and tasks to be performed in a routinely manner. Anything that takes control over their daily actions makes them feel suffocated or imprisoned.

27. Prone to putting on weight without overeating - The extra weight serves as another layer of protection to prevent the incoming negative energies from creating much impact.

28. Intolerant of narcissism - Empaths are kind, appreciative and highly tolerant of other people. Even so, they do not like being around exceedingly egotistical individuals who always put themselves first and are inconsiderate of other people's feelings and points of view.

29. Senses the energy of food - Empaths commonly refuse to eat meat and poultry products because they can sense the vibrations of the animals, especially if the animals suffered. That's why

you'll often encounter an empath who is either a vegan or a vegetarian.

30. Feels the days of the week - Empaths can pick up the feeling of the collective, enabling them to distinguish between days of the week only through their senses. For instance, the first couple days of a long holiday weekend (say Thanksgiving or Easter) can feel as if the world is calm, relaxed and smiling. Monday, Tuesday and Sunday evenings have a heavy feeling, while Friday is lighter and more laid-back.

31. Chooses not to buy second-hand, vintage, or antique items - Anything that has been previously owned carries the vibration or energy of its former owner. This is why empaths mostly prefer to buy a newly built house or a brand new car, more so if they have the financial capacity.

32. Can appear shy, moody and disconnected - The face an empath shows to the world depends on how he/she is currently feeling. Empaths can be susceptible to terrible mood swings. If they have taken on too much negativity, they may appear quiet, aloof, dissociated and, at times, even miserable. Empaths do not like pretending to be happy when they are sad or depressed, as it only makes their load heavier.

33. Has a huge heart and sometimes gives too much - Empaths have big hearts and they always try to ease the pain of other people: a distraught loved one, a broken-hearted friend, a hurt child, a homeless person, etc. It is a natural urge for them to reach out to those people and free them from pain. Most of the time, though, empaths tend to absorb too much of the pain and end up being the one feeling exhausted and fed up.

If all or most of the above traits check out, then you are most likely an empath. There are pros and cons to being an empath and you should learn and master the ropes so that you can make the most out of the pros and avoid or overcome the cons.

Chapter 3 - Surviving Emotional Vampires

Emotional vampires are people who feed off your psychic or emotional energy, making you feel angry, defensive, depressed, depleted or completed drained after you've been with them. They are everywhere, wearing many disguises and hiding behind different masks.

An emotional vampire can be anyone: your friend, an acquaintance, a family member, your boss, a co-worker, and even your kids or romantic partner. People who exhibit the traits of an emotional vampire generally lack sensitivity, empathy and emotional maturity. They feel a sense of insecurity and pain inside. In attempt to heal it, they prey on the vitality of other people.

If you fall victim to these energy drainers, you may develop unhealthy symptoms and behaviors, such as depression, mood swings, isolation, overeating and feeling fatigue. The worst part is that sometimes, no matter how much you want to cut these negative people out, you just really can't avoid them.

While you can't steer clear of these vampires, you can use self-defense techniques to reduce their negative effects on you. Below are 7 kinds of emotional vampires you are likely to come into contact with, and some friendly advice to defend yourself and nurture your energy.

1. The Narcissist

Narcissists always put themselves first and want everything to be about them and only them. They hog attention, crave admiration and have an exaggerated sense of entitlement and self-importance. They are not capable of showing genuine interest and empathy towards other people. They constantly expect you to do as they say, feed their egos and put them on top of every list.

If you refuse to do what they say, they become cold, punishing and withholding. Narcissists also have a way of manipulating you with pretentious charm then quickly turning their backs and betraying you. If you're around a narcissist vampire, you may feel extremely disempowered as they crush you underneath their limelight.

How to Defend Yourself

Because of their "Me first" motto, declaring your needs or getting angry at a narcissist will not make any difference. They are emotionally limited, so give up the idea that they can change into a selfless, caring and supportive person. Never confide your innermost thoughts and feelings to them or make them determine your worth.

If possible, cut a narcissist vampire out of your life. If not,—perhaps he or she is a relative or an unavoidable classmate or co-worker—then limit your contact as much as possible.

2. The Victim

A victim preys off your guilt and grates on you with his "poor me" attitude. He thinks the world is against him and suffers primarily because of other people. Victim vampires have no capacity to take responsibility for their lives, and instead they manipulate, emotionally blackmail and continually blame other people for their misery.

When you recommend a solution to their problems, victims will respond, "Yes, but..." Without constantly showing them signs of appreciation, love and approval, they feel unacceptable and unworthy, which they attempt to resolve by sucking out your empathy/sympathy and making you feel guilty.

How to Defend Yourself:

Set firm limitations without appearing rude. Listen briefly to their complaints or tales of woe, then breathe and reply by saying something like, "I hope things will work out," or "It must be terrible to feel that way." Then, let them know you have other things to take care of and excuse yourself politely.

You can also give non-verbal cues such as breaking eye contact or crossing your arms to make them realize you have no time to listen any further. Do not act as their therapist, financial consultant or matchmaker. Minimize your interaction with them and limit your calls to once per week.

3. The Constant Talker

Constant talkers aren't concerned about your feelings. They are only concerned about their own. They tell you random, unending stories as if there was no tomorrow. You wait for them to give an opening for you to get a word out, but they never do. They may even physically move in close to you that they're almost breathing on your face. Each time you step backwards, they edge even closer.

How to Defend Yourself

These vampires do not respond to non-verbal cues, so you must interrupt and speak up as toughly as necessary. Listen to their stories for a few minutes then cut them politely by saying, "I hate to cut you off, but there are other things I need to attend to".

Saying something in this context is more constructive than telling them to keep quiet or that they're driving you crazy. If it's a close friend or a family member, respond with "I'd appreciate if you gave me a chance to talk so I could add to this conversation". Say it in a neutral manner so you can be better heard.

4. The Controller / Dominator

These individuals have an obsession of controlling you and dictating how you are supposed to feel and become. They have opinions about everything and lecture you on current world issues, lifestyle choices, parenting decisions, and so forth. They tell you what they believe is best for you and leave you feeling demeaned, dominated and deprecated.

Controller vampires tend to act like an alpha male or female. They purposely intimidate you and invalidate your emotions when they aren't in accordance with their rule book. These vampires are often loud-mouthed individuals who hold rigid beliefs and perceive the world as black and white.

How to Defend Yourself

Agree to disagree. Never attempt to control a controller or it will only prove fruitless. Practice healthy assertiveness and do not throw their lectures back at them. Respond politely by saying, "I appreciate your advice but I prefer to handle this issue myself". Understand that their attempt to intimidate or dominate you may be due to their fear of being the one who's dominated and hurt. Be confident in conversing with them and never fall victim.

5. The Melodramatic

The melodramatic has a flair for creating "grave" problems out of the most trivial incidents. Often, their need for constant drama is a result of dark underlying hollowness in their lives. They love to seek out crisis as it gives them reasons to feel abused or victimized, thus in need of special love and attention. Melodramatic vampires are self-important individuals who constantly find ways to avoid real life issues. Another reason they enjoy making drama is because they feed off negative emotions that are addictive, like anger and pessimism.

How to Defend Yourself

When dealing with a melodramatic, remain calm and take deep breaths. This will prevent you from getting caught up in their theatrical. Set firm but kind limits. For example, if the vampire is your employee who always comes late to work due to minor health concerns or parking issues, tell him or her: "Sorry to hear about your mishaps, but you must come on time if you want to keep your job". Create distance if possible. If you can afford to cut the vampire entirely out of your life, then by all means, do so.

6. The Criticizer / Judgmental

The criticizers or judgmental vampires are individuals with severely low self-image who enjoy picking on other people. How they treat others merely reflects the treatment they give to themselves. To bolster their ego, these vampires belittle you, prey on your insecurities, and make you feel small, ashamed and pathetic. This can be your boss who shakes his head while telling you that you still have A LOT to work on, or a co-worker who always pins downs the littlest flaws in your appearance.

How to Defend Yourself

Do not take what these vampires say personally. Remember: true self-worth comes from within. Never get defensive and express appreciation for what is useful. If you receive a misplaced criticism, you may address it by saying, "I'd appreciate if you can give constructive criticism that is specific to my job". Be aware of these people's deep pain and need to feel better about themselves. Give them a compliment if you're benefitting from their experience and proficiency. Remain kind and sweet - that will really throw them off balance.

7. The Innocent

Emotional vampires are not always spiteful, as in the case of the innocents. These can sometimes be the helpless type of people who truly need your help, like close friends or children who cannot take care of themselves yet. While it's good that you lend a hand to those you genuinely care about, it is also important that you raise their spirits and encourage them to be a more self-sufficient person. Acting as their constant "tower of strength" will eventually wear your energy away. As a result, you will have little energy to help yourself.

How to Defend Yourself

Helping people in need is a representation of love and compassion, but you also need to love and protect yourself. Be there when they need you, but avoid draining your energy in comforting or saving them. Gently remind them that you also need time to care for yourself. Encourage the innocent vampires in your life to develop resilience, strength and fortitude so you can move on from being their constant giver or caretaker.

To increase your energy levels and enrich your relationships, take an inventory of the people who drain your energy and those who reenergize you. Spend time with loving and nurturing people, and set boundaries with those who leave you feeling used and exhausted. This will ultimately improve the quality of your life.

Chapter 4 - Understanding Psychic Empaths

There are different kinds of empaths who specialize in specific types of psychic work. Geomancy is a skill in which the empath senses the energies and vibrations of the earth. You can use this skill in dousing, detecting water underground, or predicting upcoming bad weather. Psychometry is the psychic ability, which enables an empath to obtain impressions from various objects. This is sometimes used by the police in solving strange or violent crimes.

Clair cognizance is another unique skill in which the empath knows exactly what measures to take or actions to perform in any given situation, especially during an emergency or a crisis. They can act with self-assurance, peace and calmness, inspiring everyone around them to act in the same way.

Some empaths can also sense spirits and work with them, a psychic ability called mediumship. Some can heal by feeling other people's symptoms and help them by transmuting energies. Similarly, they can help others overcome emotional traumas. Some empaths can communicate with nature in general while others do the same with animals. Precognition is another rare gift in which psychic empaths can perceive events or disasters that are about to occur.

While empaths are endowed with significant abilities as mentioned above, they often pay a high price for these. Often, they are being judged and misunderstood. Sometimes, they also receive derogative, even contemptuous, remarks for their declarations. Empaths can be particularly sensitive of their environment, causing them to acquire physical up-sets and strange allergies that cannot be diagnosed by regular medical practitioners.

Although their talents and abilities are truly significant, they are not all-knowing. Their skills may not work at optimum levels all the time, nor can they heal all ills and diseases of mankind.

History of Psychic Empaths

Since prehistoric times, psychics played a notable role in human culture. They often hold positions as priests, priestesses, seers and mystics in various religions prior to the inception of Christianity.

Many psychic seers can be found in the Bible, including Samuel, Gad and Amos. Samuel was the one who found the donkey of King Saul. Gad was King David's personal seer, while Amos was the seer commanded by Amaziah to escape Judah and practice his prophetic endeavors outside that land.

One of the most recognized names in ancient psychics is the Greek Oracle of Delphi. It wasn't an actual person, but rather an office convened by the cleverest woman in Delphi. She interpreted information directly from Apollo, the God of Light and Truth. Her visions were increased by the natural steams emanating from the hot springs in the Delphi area. In ancient Egypt, the well-known seers were the priests of Ra on Memphis. In Assyria, oracles were called *nabu*, meaning "announce" or "to call."

During the Renaissance period in France, Nostradamus became a famous name in prophesying. His prophesies are still well-recognized across the globe and have been on print consistently since they were first written.

In mid-1800s, when the planet Neptune was discovered (a discovery that rules psychics), the Spiritualist Movement began and expanded. Many psychics flourished during that period, including Edgar Cayce, Daniel Dunglas Home, and Madame Blavatsky.

Psychic empaths have walked the Earth ever since the dawning of humankind's history. However, it was only during the New Age Awakening of the 70s and 80s that empathic skills were recognized as being distinct from other psychics.

How Empaths Feel

Since empaths are highly sensitive to the different energies surrounding them, they often fall victim to inner conflict and tremendous stress. When an empath's empathetic nature is in full effect, he may experience abnormal nervousness or feel as if an electrical current is suddenly overpowering him. This is followed by an overflow of emotions.

Strong melancholic feelings may arise out of nowhere and engulf him. This can become confusing for the empath since he may not completely understand what's happening to him. He takes on those feelings as his own and tries to formulate an explanation as to why he feels such unfounded emotions.

Because of this, it is no surprise that most empaths become terribly depressed at some point of their life. Depression may even be a recurring visitor for many of them. Besides negative emotions, empaths can also absorb other people's positive vibrations. However, this up-and-down phenomenon can create an emotional rollercoaster ride for the untrained, unaware and inexperienced empath.

How Empaths Obtain Information

The true mechanisms of psychic/empathic abilities are still unknown. Numerous theories have been made in an attempt to explain such mechanisms, but all of it were mere matters of conjecture. Not all empaths possess only one ability. Some can obtain information using multiple psychic skills that work in unison to create one "mega" psychic ability.

For instance, an empath may use his psychometric abilities to obtain information by simply touching a person or an object. Then, his empathic ability processes that information to induce feelings. Looking beyond those two psychic abilities, the empath may also possess strong clairaudience, clairvoyance, and other skills that facilitate the processing of all the information he is receiving.

It can be difficult for a psychic empath to find ways to control the information he receives until he stops to evaluate his individual processes and determine if he is operating only on empathic abilities or a set of abilities. Testing oneself on each potential ability requires a great deal of patience and time. However, once the empath has successfully established a baseline, it will be much easier to comprehend how his individual psychic ability is related and how his combined abilities function and interact.

Chapter 5 - Shielding & Clearing your Energy

Shielding means protecting yourself against negative, harsh, and lower energies. It is a way to make sure that your energy remains clean and high, especially when you're working in or travelling through a harsh environment. Below are some of the most effective ways to shield your energy:

Crystals and Gemstones

Crystals are powerful stones, rocks and minerals that can protect, magnify and transmute various energies. Holding, wearing, sleeping or working near these protective gemstones help repel negative energy and enhance positivity. Some of the most effective shielding crystals are the following:

Amethyst

This beautiful purple gemstone is excellent for protection and purification. It enhances intuition, helps release addictions, improves spiritual awareness and lifts the energy in you and around you. At the same time, it wards off negative energy - both ethereal and spiritual. Having this crystal around will greatly help you in coping with your empathic abilities.

Blue Topaz

This crystal will help you think clearly and ease the tension brought about by your work, social or love life. It will also help you communicate your thoughts, desires and pleas to the universe, and see the bigger picture.

Black Tourmaline

This powerful protection gemstone is particularly helpful for empathic healers. It fends off all negative energy, including those that are being purposefully directed at an individual and general negative energy coming from the world around you.

Green Aventurine

This crystal possesses great vitality, making it an excellent healing stone for any situation related to health, friends, finances, growth, confidence and everything else. This is an important stone to have in an empath's arsenal.

Obsidian

Wearing this gorgeous black gemstone will help you ground yourself. It deflects anger, psychic attacks and negativity.

Citrine

This stone represents happiness and creativity. If you're feeling down or stuck in a creative block, this lovely yellow stone can definitely help you. It gives a powerful boost for all things related to finances, abundance and prosperity. It also manifests radiant energy, which pushes away negativity and attracts positive vibes.

Lepidolite

Lepidolite enhances the power of other nearby stones and crystals, and relieves anxieties that commonly plague empaths. This stone is well-known for its peace, power and ability to foster love, luck and sleep.

Malachite

Malachite is perfect if you want to eliminate emotional blockages and pressures that may occur when dealing with stressful situations. This gemstone has a great tendency to absorb negative emotions you may be keeping inside.

Rose Quartz

The energy of this pale pink crystal is really gentle, calm and compassionate. It provides a feeling of genuine, unconditional love, and protects you in romantic relationships. It also heals and soothes the heart chakra, and pushes away all the negative feelings around you.

Clear Quartz

This stone is highly versatile and can act as a powerful amplifier of any frequency, including the natural electromagnetic frequency (EMF) in the human body. This clear crystal can refract sunlight into rainbows, and deflect negative energy and vibrations.

Smoky Quartz

This crystal releases negativity from your past relationships. Place it close to your bed and let it do its job while you sleep. You will wake feeling lighter and with a more positive outlook.

Lapis Lazuli

This stunning blue stone is another excellent protector, but its influence is more inclined to spiritual growth. It helps you maintain an objective attitude and take others' actions lightly and not too personally. This stone helps keep your energy unbound and your mind clear of muddled thoughts, great for use in the office or other workplaces.

Jade

This is a popular crystal amongst lovers, but is great for empaths, too. Jade helps balance the opposing energies of romantic partners, and prevent them from inflicting harm on themselves and others during spats and quarrels.

Turquoise

Turquoise drives negative energy out of your space and creates a stronger, more resilient bond between your physical body and energy field. Even a small piece of this stone can go a long way, filling an entire home with positive vibrations and soothing energy. Many people consider turquoise as the ultimate anti-negativity gemstone.

Unakite

Although not as popular as the other stones, Unakite can be a great inclusion in your arsenal. This crystal helps balance your emotions and bring your spirit close to the other side so that you can stay connected to late loved ones who may be checking on you every once in a while.

Zoiste:

Zoiste is another uncommon yet valuable crystal. It is perfect for artistic empaths because it promotes creativity, individuality and connectedness to other people. Many artistic empaths are introverted and tend to shut everybody out. This stone reminds the spirit that human contact is not only important, but can also be fun.

Fossils

While not exactly a crystal or gemstone, fossils are also important to an empath's wellbeing. Fossils will keep you strong and grounded, and constantly remind you that energy is fluid and everything will change inevitably.

Picking the Perfect Crystals

After deciding on what crystals you need, you will then have to pick out the right ones. Certain stones work better for some, but not as well for others. Follow these three steps to find the perfect crystals for you.

1. Set your intention.

Before you begin the process of finding the perfect gemstone or crystal, you must first set an intention. Speak inside yourself or aloud about what crystal you're hoping to find. Example: "Amethyst, thank you for becoming my new crystal. Please show yourself to me."

2. Follow your senses.

As empaths, we have strong intuitive senses and physical senses. Intuitive senses include Clair cognizance (clear knowing), clairgustance (clear tasting), clairalience (clear smelling), clairsentience (clear feeling), clairaudience (clear hearing), and clairvoyance (clear seeing). Turn on all of these senses when picking your perfect gemstone.

3. Wait for a feeling.

There are times when a gemstone or crystal just stands out among the others. If you come across a stone, which keeps grabbing your attention, then that might be the one for you. Also, some crystals vibrate or emit a certain kind of energy when handled by the right person. Wait for that feeling.

Angelic Shielding

You can appeal to the protector Archangel Michael to protect you with his royal purple and royal blue light. Say this either silently or aloud, *"Archangel Michael, please shield me with your protective light now."* This archangel is limitless, so can instantly protect anyone who calls on him.

You can also call upon God and ask Him to send additional guardian angels to look after you, your home, your loved ones, your friends, or any other important person, thing or place. Angels are infinite in number, and all you need to do is ask and more will come for you.

Clearing

Clearing your energy is as important as shielding it. Whenever you get confused, feel exhausted, or become prone to accidents, take a break to clear your energy. Most of the time, these are signs that you have absorbed too much negativity.

Like shielding, there are different ways to clear yourself and this also includes calling upon Archangel Michael. You can say: *"Archangel Michael, I ask of you to clear away all the energies within and around me that aren't of God's light and love."* The archangel instantly comes to the aid of everyone who calls on him, for he loves all of us and has the capacity to help everyone at once.

Another fine way to clear your energy is to take a warm bath enhanced by Epsom salts (sea salts are fine) and essential oils. You can further improve it by adding pure flower essences to your bathwater and surrounding your tub with white candles. The candles will serve as focal points for your genuine intention of clearing yourself.

Massage and similar bodyworks also have excellent clearing abilities, especially if your massage therapist is skilled in relieving physical tension and energy.

Detoxing and tweaking your diet is another effective way to dispel energetic and physical toxins. You can work with juices, supplements or herbs that flush out contaminants and heavy metals attached to the energy toxins in your system. Consult a naturopath or a trained staff at your local supplements store to get the best recommendations.

Grounding

Grounding means your consciousness is contained inside your body, instead of floating freely above it. Many empaths leave their physical bodies when the earth plane becomes too much to handle. They "go home" inside their consciousness and you can say they are not really "here." It is okay to do this during meditation or dream time, but during your waking hours, remember the reasons you are in your physical body.

Besides wearing obsidian crystal to help you ground yourself, eat organic, non-GMO vegetables such as turnips, onions, carrots, potatoes and radishes. You can also get a foot rub or visualize yourself as a tree, with roots growing out of your feet. Feel the earth's energy connect with the bottom of your feet.

Another way to ground yourself is to connect physically with nature. Take your shoes off and touch the soil, sand, grass or water. This will help you shift your focus back to your physical reality.

Conclusion

Thank you again for downloading this book!

I hope this book was able to help you understand the empathic nature much better and give you clear-cut techniques on how to shield your energy from harsh environments. You have had these amazing qualities in you all this time. Perhaps you were unaware or wasn't sure how to deal with them. And now, hopefully you already are. Whenever you feel like you're getting off track again, remember to refresh yourself on the useful contents of this book.

As with other great powers, empathic powers also come with great responsibility and consequences. It's up to you to decide how you will use your abilities to make this world a better place to live in.

Finally, if you enjoyed this book and found it helpful, then I'd like to ask you for a favor. Would you be kind enough to leave a review for this book on Amazon? This feedback will help me continue to write the kind of Kindle books that help you get results.

Thank you and good luck!

Similar Books by this Author:

TWK-Publishing.com

Non-Fiction:

Psychic: The Beginner Guide to Psychic development to increase your psychic abilities.

http://geni.us/tFQR

Speed Reading: Become the top 1% of reader in the world and dramatically increase your speed reading.

http://geni.us/xzsIAT

**The Power of Focus:
How to Beat Procrastination and achieve more.**

http://geni.us/KaCpv

**Sleep Smarter, Not Harder:
How to Sleep Your Way to Wealth and Happiness.**

http://geni.us/CSC1n

Ultimate Morning Rituals:
A plan to conquer the morning to feel more alive and gain more success in life.

http://geni.us/4CS2

Ketosis Diet Explained:
Eat Fat, Be Thin, and Seven steps to a low-carb ketosis diet. Transform your body fast.

http://geni.us/38ly

eBay Arbitrage:
Earn Risk Free Money without Investment. 5 Steps to make Risk Free Money without investment.

http://geni.us/1PIL

YouTube Profits:
No Filming, No Money Needed Secrets Revealed. Be anywhere and make Big Profits.

http://geni.us/2Rah

Made in the USA
Middletown, DE
06 May 2017